Routledge Revivals

Children's Dreams

Children's Dreams

C. W. Kimmins

Routledge
Taylor & Francis Group

First published in 1920 by Longmans, Green and Co. Ltd.

This edition first published in 2018 by Routledge
2 Park Square, Milton Park, Abingdon, Oxon, OX14 4RN
and by Routledge
52 Vanderbilt Avenue, New York, NY 10017, USA

Routledge is an imprint of the Taylor & Francis Group, an informa business

© 1920 Taylor & Francis

Publisher's Note
The publisher has gone to great lengths to ensure the quality of this reprint but points out that some imperfections in the original copies may be apparent.

Disclaimer
The publisher has made every effort to trace copyright holders and welcomes correspondence from those they have been unable to contact.
A Library of Congress record exists under ISBN:

ISBN 13: 978-0-367-10941-7 (hbk)
ISBN 13: 978-0-367-10949-3 (pbk)
ISBN 13: 978-0-429-02405-4 (ebk)

HARDPRESS

ISBN: 9781290742498

Published by:
HardPress Publishing
8345 NW 66TH ST #2561
MIAMI FL 33166-2626

Email: info@hardpress.net
Web: http://www.hardpress.net

CHILDREN'S DREAMS

CHILDREN'S DREAMS

BY

C. W. KIMMINS, M.A., D.Sc.

LONGMANS, GREEN AND CO.

39 PATERNOSTER ROW, LONDON

FOURTH AVENUE & 30TH STREET, NEW YORK

BOMBAY, CALCUTTA, AND MADRAS

1920

TO

MY WIFE

PREFACE

THE dream of the neurotic has in recent years attained a position of very considerable importance in the diagnosis of war neuroses and a large variety of nervous disorders. Very little attention has, however, been given to the dreams of normal healthy children, and the investigation which forms the basis of the material of this little volume is wholly concerned with the latter type.

It will be noticed that in the records of dreams of the younger children they have been, in some cases, woven into connected stories by a greater fusion with waking material than is common in the dreams of adults. It was thought that some children had invented dreams, but an attempt to obtain "faked" narratives by essays written on imaginary dreams proved that such material can readily be distinguished from the true records, and there was no difficulty in eliminating dreams of this nature.

The important part played by the unconscious in the child's normal behaviour is now fully recognised, and the dream as the best means of obtaining valuable evidence of the content of the unconscious opens up a rich field of useful research.

The analysis simply attempts a rough classification of the type of dream peculiar to children of different ages, showing the variation from year to year and the influence of environment. The large number of dreams investigated makes the conclusions reliable within this limited sphere and points the way to a more detailed and thorough investigation. The educational possibilities of such a fascinating line of enquiry are unlimited.

I must tender my sincere thanks to many friends who have assisted me in the collection of dreams, and especially to Mr. Cyril Burt for many valuable suggestions in regard to the method of conducting the investigation.

CONTENTS

CHILDREN'S DREAMS

CHAPTER I

INTRODUCTION

THE dream has from time immemorial been regarded with intense interest. In the sacred writings, the man who could interpret dreams was regarded with very special reverence, as being endowed with a power withheld from the ordinary mortal. Throughout the ages, the dream, with its atmosphere of mystery and frequently terrifying associations has been an object of wonder and has fascinated the investigator. It is only of recent years, however, that the value of the dream has been fully recognised as an important factor in the diagnosis of difficult cases of nervous breakdown. Among the human wreckage caused by the Great War, the interpreter of dreams in shell-shock hospitals has been of the greatest possible assistance in the investigation of war neuroses. In many instances, complete recovery has resulted from treatment based on a diagnosis of the mental trouble which has been revealed by the interpretation of the dreams of the sufferer.

With such a fascinating objective as that of the unravelling of dreams, it is only natural that when psychology joined the rank of the experimental sciences, expert investigators should be attracted to this particular field of research. Of these investigators, the most distinguished are Freud, the leader of the Vienna School, and Jung, the leader of the Zurich School.

According to Freud, what is known as the unconscious consists almost entirely of material which has been repressed because it is painful and repulsive to consciousness. This suppressed material may eventually become so dissociated from the normal content of consciousness that the ordinary laws of association have not the power of recalling it, as in the case of ordinary facts and experiences which are not repulsive to consciousness. To prevent the passage of the contents of the unconscious into the state of consciousness, there is a well-ordered mental adjustment, which Freud personifies under the name of the censor.

In the sleeping condition, however, the censor is less alert than in the normal waking state, and in dreams, material in a disguised form, a sort of camouflage, which makes it appear unoffensive, enables some of it to get through from unconsciousness to consciousness. The expert knowledge of the investigator enables him, by removing the camouflage, to lay bare the true material as it exists in the unconscious, and herein lies the skill of the interpreter of dreams. A dream which appears to the layman simply an absurd jumble of irrelevant material now becomes something which is full of meaning.

Opinions are divided as to the content of the unconscious. Jung maintains, and in this he is supported by many competent observers, that Freud over-stresses the part played by suppressed material of an unpleasant nature. He claims that the content is much richer, and contains instinctive elements which have become useless in our present state of civilisation but which may be of great value in the important crises of life and may come to our aid in overwrought and nervous states. The whole problem of the unconscious has recently received a great amount of attention, and has been so ably treated by distinguished psychologists that a most interesting and valuable mass of literature has resulted, in which the function and interpretation of the dream have been fully discussed. The discussion has, however, naturally been especially concerned with matters of pathological interest, and has centred around the dreams of neurotic adults in connection with the treatment of war and other neuroses.

It is evident, from the very considerable measure of success which has attended the psycho-analytic method in the treatment of mental diseases, that the dream, which is the most direct avenue to the unconscious, can no longer be regarded simply as an object of wonder and mystery to which no importance should be attached. The influence of the unconscious in practically every action of the waking life is now widely recognised, and will receive far more attention in the future than it has in the past. The dreams of normal, healthy school children have received comparatively little attention at the hands of skilled investigators since the researches of such workers as Sante de Sanctis, Marie de Manaceine and Miss Calkins, and even their researches consisted chiefly of the intensive study of a few cases, some of which were of abnormal type.

As pointed out by Freud (*Traumdeutung*) and others, the dreams of children differ very materially from those of adults. The manifest content tends to become identical with the latent content. In children's dreams also, there is far more secondary elaboration than in the dreams of older people, and there is far more overflow from the experiences of the previous day, *e.g.*, a child often gratifies in the dream some desire forbidden by his parents the day before. The dreams of children have, moreover, clearer relation to their everyday temperament, *e.g.*, elaborate and fanciful dreams are common with imaginative children, nightmares are common with timid children, and vivid dreams are generally more frequent with those of unstable type.

In dreams referring to events of waking life the experiences may form an infinite number of new combinations, some of which are extraordinarily grotesque. It is these new combinations which give the dream such a bewildering, and at the same time, irresistible attraction.

In the investigation of children's dreams, which will be referred to, those of very young children were related individually to skilled observers, but all dreams of children of eight years of age and over were recorded by the dreamers themselves in response to the request: "Write a true and full account of the last dream you can remember. State your age, and also say about how long ago you had the dream you have described."

The numbers of dreams obtained from various sources were approximately—

150 boys and girls in Infants' schools, of 5, 6, and 7 years.

2000 boys in elementary schools, of 8 to 14 years of age.

2000 girls in elementary schools, of 8 to 14 years of age.

300 boys and girls in central schools, of 10 to 15 years of age.

600 girls in secondary schools, of 10 to 18 years of age.

300 boys in industrial schools, of 10 to 16 years of age.

300 girls in industrial schools, of 10 to 16 years of age.

110 boys and girls in blind schools, of 10 to 16 years of age.

140 boys and girls in deaf schools, of 10 to 16 years of age.

In spite of fear dreams, children in normal health delight in dreaming, and it is an evident pleasure to them to talk about or record their dreams. It will be seen by the children's accounts of their dreams that they have an abnormal power of graphic description of events in which they are intensely interested, such as those supplied by the dream material. This power so far exceeds their ability in ordinary essay writing on topics selected by the teacher, and is, moreover, so much in advance of their general standard of achievement, that it would

B

appear as if some fresh mental element had come into play. The matter is worthy of further investigation.

In analysing the children's dreams, the following, among other elements, have been considered: the various types of wish fulfilment and fear dreams; kinæsthetic dreams; references to fairy stories; dreams of bravery and adventure; school activities, cinemas, exciting books and death incidents; dreams in which conversations are recorded; the presence of other witnesses than the dreamer; and dreams in which the dreamer was absent.

Most of the dreams were recorded in November and December, 1918, but those from industrial schools were obtained in March and April, 1919, and those from the blind and deaf schools in June, 1919. The basis of classification was age, and not position in the school, and in the mixed schools, the boys' were separated from the girls' dreams.

An attempt was made to analyse on a similar plan the dreams of students of eighteen to twenty-two years of age, but the majority of them were so heavily camouflaged that it was impossible for anyone who was not a trained expert in psycho-analysis to deal with them satisfactorily. I have, therefore, confined my attention entirely to the dreams of school children.

CHAPTER II

THE NATURE OF THE DREAM

THE universality of the dream is in itself evidence of its biological significance.

The Dream as the Guardian of Sleep.— The definition of the dream as the guardian of sleep is increasingly accepted. On the other hand, the attempt to bring all dreams into the category of fulfilled wishes needs such an extension of the normal meaning of words that the definition of a dream as a fulfilled wish would serve no useful purpose. This is especially the case in dealing with the dreams of children.

The part played by the dream as an antidote to the monotony of life is clearly shown in the present investigation, particularly with regard to the dreams of very poor children, and those for whom life offers very little variety and opportunities for enjoyment. The dream comes in as the

Fairy Godmother and supplies to them the pleasures which the normal conditions of their lives have failed to provide. This is well illustrated by the dreams of industrial school children, who, as is pointed out, have far happier and more exciting dreams than those whose lives are full of interest and for whom the lines have fallen in pleasant places. The homeless, uncared-for child dreams of the happy home, supplied with every comfort, of rich relations from whom they receive costly presents, of continual change of scene, and, above all, of abundant success and prosperity in after life. The very elements which are so conspicuously lacking in their lives are those which figure most prominently in their dreams. The disappointments of the previous day are compensated by the wish fulfilments of the dream.

In young children there is far more overflow of the experiences of the day into the dream of the night than in the case of adults, in whom, as many observers have shown, the worries and anxieties which have filled their thoughts during waking hours find no place in their dreams. And thus again the dream acts as the guardian of sleep. Without doubt, life would be far more wearisome without dreams, and it is contended that the non-dreamer grows old more quickly than the dreamer.

Naturally, during the war there were many presentiment dreams of coming evil, as in the death of relatives of the dreamer. Even when such presentiments were confirmed, it was not infrequently stated in the record that the dream served a useful purpose in weakening the blow when the fatal news was received.

Effect of Environment on the Dream.—A certain amount of research, without very definite results, has been done on the influence of external conditions in influencing the nature of the dream. This may be divided into two classes—

(1) Where a particular stimulus causes a dream and influences its nature.

Some interesting results have been obtained in this connection in taste dreams, and those stimulated by odours.

(2) Where the general conditions are very similar, and have an effect in producing a greater similarity of dream material than is the case under normal circumstances.

As will be seen by the results obtained in this investigation in connection with the dreams of children in industrial schools, institutional life has a marked influence in affecting the type, diminishing the variety, and, in certain respects, reducing the differences between the girls' and the boys' dreams as compared with the dreams of children in ordinary schools. Of course, the greater similarity of the type of child also has an important influence. The conditions of institutional life also affect the amount of dreaming; *e.g.*, it is well known that criminals dream far more when they are in prison than when they are at liberty.

During the year 1917 I kept a careful record of my own dreams, and they were undoubtedly affected by the general condition of the environment. The more important points noticed were the following :—

(1) The dreams in a quiet room in the

country were far clearer and more vivid than those in London, with the noise of the streets in evidence during the greater part of the night, and, moreover, that with ears plugged with cotton wool in London the dreams corresponded more nearly to those in the country.

(2) Change of environment added to the frequency of dreams to a very marked extent until I became acclimatised to the new conditions.

(3) Hard mental work up to the time of going to bed seriously increased the tendency to dream.

(4) Sleeping in a badly ventilated room appeared to increase the frequency but diminish the clearness of my dreams.

The result of a heavy, indigestible meal just before retiring to rest is too well known in its effect on the dream to need any description. The blood supply to the brain in excess, as after mental work, or much reduced, as after a heavy meal, injuriously affects the tendency to interesting dreams. The normal blood supply appears to be the ideal condition.

The general impression among young children is that cheese is the source of every bad thing in dreaming, and many state that for pleasant dreams the best preparation is cocoa and bread and butter for supper. There was much evidence in the records of dreams that influenza, or any complaint involving a high temperature, has a most serious effect on the nature of the dream.

Another important instance of the influence of external conditions on the dream must be mentioned. During the years 1915–18 the air raid had an important effect on the frequency and terrifying nature of children's dreams in centres visited by hostile air-craft. The bulk of the records of dreams analysed were written, as I have pointed out elsewhere, some months after the last air raid, and dreams, except those of older children, contain few references to them, but in those of an earlier date a very large proportion of the fear dreams were seriously affected by air raids. Air-raid dreams are of no special interest ; they are mainly a description of raids in which the dreamer was an observer. In such cases the difficulty of separating the dreaming from the waking elements would be very great, and " secondary elaboration " would tend to make the dream fall into line with the events of the previous air raid actually witnessed.

It is clear from the records that the blind child suffered from air raids far more than any other type of child, and the deaf child the least of all.

The effect of the air raid upon the dream of the normal adult was slight, due partly to the principle referred to elsewhere, that matters which affect the emotional side of waking thoughts rarely trouble the adult dreamer, and partly to the fact that from the mathematical consideration that the chance of any personal inconvenience resulting from a raid to any particular dreamer, was very remote, and, therefore, did not enter the category of fears.

In looking through the records of my own dreams for 1917, although I was in central London during most of the raids, there is only one reference to air-raid experiences, and in that a comical element predominated. On one occasion, after having been kept awake for two hours by the noise associated with the raid, I had on regaining sleep a delightfully vivid, pleasant dream, absolutely unaffected by air-raid experience.

Dreams and Intelligence.—Many observers who have investigated the frequency of dreams in different classes of the community have reached the conclusion that people of well-developed intelligence dream far more than those of low culture. Agricultural labourers, ill-educated servant girls, and the lower types of criminals dream infrequently, and many have no memory of ever having had a dream. Some observers go so far as to say that, within certain limits, the frequency of dreaming among healthy people varies with the state of development of the intelligence.

In Jastrow's work on the retention of visual impressions in the dreams of blind children, it was found that of those who became blind between the ages of five and seven, some permanently retained the power of visualising scenes, and others did not, the deciding factor being the state of mental development. The character of the dream also varies in the imagery employed in its structure with the standard of intelligence of the dreamer.   The dream of the university professor is very different from that of the casual labourer.

In the case of children up to the age of seven, practically all dream, and the dull as frequently as the clever children.   At certain ages children dream less frequently than at others.   From the present investigation it appears that boys and girls of the ages of twelve and thirteen dream far less than before or afterwards.   The age of maximum dreaming is given by different observers as between twenty and twenty-five years. Generally speaking, dreams increase with the variety and activity of the intellectual life.

Cause and Effect in Dreams.—One of the most remarkable characteristics of the dream is the entire absence of the relation of cause to effect.   There is no reasoning in the dream, and nothing surprises the dreamer however inconsequent the juxtaposition of incongruous experiences.   The extraordinary fascination of a fairy story for the child is due largely to its approach to the dream in this respect. The disappearance of anything in the nature of logical sequence gives scope for an infinite variety of grouping and gives a wealth of incident impossible in the affairs of everyday life. Many good examples of this are given in the selected dreams. For example, a girl who is swimming to save a friend from drowning meets a teacher in the water, who tells her to go back to school at once, because she has been selected to take the part of Julius Cæsar in the play. Another girl, in witnessing the funeral of her brother, sees the brother attending his own funeral, and during the procession her teacher goes through her sums with her to see how many mistakes she has made in her arithmetic. For wealth of incident one section of a dream which is quoted elsewhere may be mentioned in this connection. A girl's father and mother are turned into cabbages and she prepares them for dinner. Just before putting them into the saucepan they turn again into father and mother, and ask her how she likes the aeroplane. She finds that she is in a

Handley-Page. The aeroplane vanishes, and she finds herself swimming in the sea. The other two sections of the dream are equally full of incident.

In the record of many dreams conversations are given, but these are lacking in interest. Compared with the imagery, the grotesqueness and irrational grouping of incidents, the conversation, which obeys a certain logical order, appears commonplace. It is natural also that secondary elaboration should play more havoc with conversations than with the description of the other parts of the dream in bringing them more into touch with normal methods of speech. The absence of spatial relations adds to the weird sequence of events in the dream. The dreamer passes from the surroundings of the home to far distant scenes, has a variety of adventures and in an incredibly short space of time finds himself at home again. The change of the dreamer into animals, which occurs more frequently at certain ages than at others, is an additional element in separating the dream from any other type of experience.

The Kinæsthetic Dream. — The great

variety of falling sensations, gliding, floating in the air or water, often accompanied by loss of muscular and speech control, are here included in the term Kinæsthetic Dream. The various explanations given of the cause of this type of dream are far from satisfactory. From the present investigation it appears—

(1) That children under the age of nine or ten years rarely experience it.

(2) That from ten years of age it increases in frequency fairly steadily up to the age of seventeen or eighteen.

(3) That well-fed children are more subject to it than those living under less favourable conditions.

(4) That regular institutional life tends to diminish this type of dream very considerably.

(5) That the deaf child scarcely ever has a kinæsthetic dream.

(6) That children who have had influenza or any type of malady accompanied by high temperature are particularly susceptible to it.

The differences between boys and girls

of different ages in connection with the frequency and type of this kind of dream are discussed elsewhere.

The Book and the Dream.—There is abundant evidence that the dream of the child is much affected by the reading of an exciting book just before going to sleep. This type of dream has very definite characteristics of its own, and may not be so trustworthy in consequence of the obvious difficulty of separating the book story from the dream story. The child nearly always assumes the most attractive character in the book, not necessarily of the same sex, and the changes effected in the dream are sometimes very interesting, and if the dream could definitely be relied upon, might throw a light upon the dreamer's character by the over-emphasis of certain qualities of the hero or heroine.

Some children have a remarkable power of condensation and of giving an excellent abstract of a story in the dream. In other cases the general plot serves as a structure for a dream containing much material having no connection with the real story.

The book influences the blind child's dream far more than that of other children, and the dreamer does not always take a part, but simply acts as the passive observer witnessing the unfolding of the story. The blind child generally has a far more accurate knowledge of the details of a book than the seeing child.

The Variation of the Type of Dream with Age.—As will be seen by the results of the analysis of children's dreams, the content of the dream varies from age to age in the type of wish fulfilment, fear, main interest, and other particulars. It varies also with the state of health of the child. Certain elements appear practically at the same age with groups of children, and others disappear in equally regular order. A comparative study of wish fulfilments is most illuminating in showing the change of interest as age increases.

A series of dreams of the same child, recorded within a short time of each other, although they contain a variety of very different material, have certain characteristics of a constant nature which enter into the

C

constitution of each dream and afford an excellent clue not only to the child's chief interests, but give a certain amount of evidence as to the type of mental make-up to which it belongs.

Interpretation of Dreams.—The large amount of attention which has been given of recent years to the dreams of neurotics, together with the universal recognition of the great value of the dream in connection with the treatment of nervous diseases, has resulted, as has been pointed out, in a vast increase in our knowledge of dealing with the material of the unconscious.

It would be a great mistake to apply the methods which have proved so successful in these pathological cases to the dreams of normal, healthy children, though they may be of considerable value in investigating difficult cases among school children of un-stable type, who do not respond to ordinary methods of instruction. The dream of the normal child may be invaluable in many directions, but it should always be borne in mind that the problem is a different one from the investigation of the dream of the neurotic.

There is unquestionably a rich field for research in connection with the dreams of normal children, which may yield a harvest as abundant in educational procedure as that obtained by psycho-analysis in the realm of pathology.

CHAPTER III

DREAMS OF CHILDREN OF FIVE, SIX, AND SEVEN YEARS OF AGE

IN the Infants' schools, apart from a few written records by clever children of seven years of age, the dreams were told to the head mistresses individually, and not in the presence of other children, to avoid all possibility of suggestion.

In dealing with the dreams of very young children, both in spoken and written records, there are many difficulties which must be borne in mind in estimating the value of the results.

The more important of these are—

1. That young children have great difficulty in separating the dreaming from the waking element.

2. That their powers of description are

naturally very limited, and that their use of words may convey to the adult mind a very different impression from that which they wish to convey.

3. That the child will inevitably fill up gaps in the dream, and will reject as absurd some items in the dream which are contrary to his own experience.

4. A dream described even a few hours after awaking would be a very different record from that obtained directly the child awoke, in consequence of the fusion of the dream material with waking thoughts.

Anything, therefore, in the nature of a full analysis of a young child's dream would be valueless.   All that can be done is to classify the dream elements into definite groups.

Analysis of Dreams of Children of Five, Six, and Seven Years of Age

1. *Fulfilled Wishes.*—Dreams of this nature consisted very largely in the return of father, brother and near relations from the war, more particularly in the girls' dreams.   Prospective dreams of Christmas with Santa Claus and his presents figured very largely, especially with the five-year-old children, reaching, in

fact, 15 per cent. of the total dream elements at this age. Infant school children dream far less about food than those in the senior departments.

2. *Fears.*—With very young children the fear dream is very prominent. In this investigation, no less than 25 per cent. were of this nature, consisting chiefly of the dread of objectionable men. At seven years of age children, both boys and girls, dream more about burglars than at any other age. The fear dream of animals is, curiously enough, far more common among the boys than the girls.

3. *School Activities*, as such, appear very little in the dreams of children of any age. In the Infants' schools only about 1 per cent. are of this nature.

4. *Air-raid Dreams* only occur to the extent of about 4 per cent., due, no doubt, to the interval of about seven months between the last raid and the time of the records.

5. *The Influence of the Cinema* is felt very little in the girls' dreams, but in the boys', especially at the age of seven, it is an important factor.

6. *Fairy-story Dreams* are very common with girls, but are rarely experienced by boys.

7. *Normal Domestic Occurrences* appear frequently in the material of the girls' dreams, but only occasionally in those of the boys.

The more important facts which emerge from the consideration of the dreams of the children in Infants' schools are the following:—

1. The passing of the ghost and the coming of the fairy. The ghost, which was in days gone by the terror of the dreaming child, has almost entirely disappeared. There was only one reference to a ghost in 338 dream elements in the Infants' schools under consideration. The fairy dream is generally one of pure enjoyment, the only objectionable feature is the witch; this, however, is a comparatively rare occurrence.

2. At five years of age, the child is the centre of the dream, and is rarely a passive observer. Family relationships are not fully realised. There are many incongruities which will be seen by the following dreams:—

(*a*) A burglar came into my house and stole Mother's money. He stuck a knife into me, and I dreamt that he had shot another boy after he had killed me.

(*b*) I dreamt that a robber came to our house and broke the cups. (This boy had broken a cup and concealed the matter from his mother. This is an interesting case of repressed material at an early age.)

(*c*) A tiger came to our house and ate Mummy and Daddy and my brother and me, and then I woke up and cried and said "It isn't true."

(*d*) I dreamt that teacher was married in a church, and the church had flowers all over, and the gas was alight. Teacher went into a motor car and had a nice tea party.

(*e*) Someone came and took our white baby and left a black one.

(*f*) I dreamt we had a party because Daddy had come home, and we had a violin, and a gramophone played all the evening.

(*g*) After the visit of the King and Queen to Peckham, a girl of five dreamt that "a lady was sitting on my bed, and the King and Queen were under the bed eating bread and butter, and a lot of ladies with them."

3. At the age of five, the experiences of conscious life carry over into the unconscious. The child mixes up the dreaming with the waking elements.

4. At the age of seven, there is a great advance. The family relationship is fully realised, and members of the family group take part in the dream. The child is not so much the central figure. At this age, he recognises the dream phenomenon as a thing apart. There is also less confusion between the dreaming and the waking experiences, and the record of the dream becomes much more valuable.

A few examples of the dreams of children of this age will illustrate this:—

(*a*) The sun and moon were on the floor in my room, so that I could not walk about, and so I went to heaven where all the lights were up, and there were many colours.

(*b*) I dreamt a dustman put me in a box and took me in a cart, and brought me back to the wrong bed, but when I woke up, I was in the right bed.

(*c*) I dreamt there were burglars in the room and they lit the fire and sat in a chair, and got green curtains by the door. There were flowers in the next-door garden; the burglars took them and they gave me two stamps and a sheet of paper.

(*d*) I went to my aunty's and she gave me some biscuits; we had a tea party and a soldier on crutches came in and he said to my aunty " Have a waltz."

5. The dream appears to vary with the sex, temperament and health of the child. A careful record of the dreams of children, especially those of a neurotic type, throughout the year, would be very valuable.

6. Children in poor districts dream far more about toys than those in the well-to-do.

7. There appears to be no connection of dreaming with intelligence, though this appears later. Dull children dream quite as much as bright children.

8. The dreams of young children are vivid and very real. A boy of six dreamt that someone had given him a threepenny piece, and on waking, searched the bed for it.

9. The death element comes into the dreams of delicate, neurotic children, but rarely into those of healthy, normal children.

10. The rare dreams of school activities are generally associated with the playground rather than the classroom.

11. Dreams of bravery and adventure, which are common in the senior school, rarely come into the dreams of those in the Infants' school. Here is an exception :—

A boy of seven dreamt that " I was an

American soldier, and I had an army of soldiers, and we went into Germany and we captured the Kaiser and Little Willie."

12. Young children sometimes imagine that they take other forms ; *e. g.*—

A nervous boy of five, whose father was a baker, had two dreams of this character :

(*a*) I was in a loaf of bread, and a German cut it into little bits, and saw me ; I flew away—I had wings on me.

(*b*) I was in a kettle, and I drank up all the water.   Mother could not find me ; I went under the gas-pipes.

One boy of five dreamt he was a little girl ; another of the same age, that he was a horse.

13. Kinæsthetic (movement) elements are uncommon in the dreams of very young children.   They appear generally at about ten years of age, and become very vivid and frequent at the ages of eleven and twelve.

Young children's dreams are much simpler than those of adults, even when full allowance has been made for the inevitable simplification produced in the course of the child's narrative owing to the limitation of vocabulary and descriptive accuracy. They are not so clearly marked off by an atmosphere of unreality and, moreover, they are not infrequently reported as actual occurrences.

According to Freud, the unfulfilled wishes of the day preceding are insufficient to produce a dream in adults. In young children, on the other hand, the dream is often much concerned with the events of yesterday. Retrospective dreams, however, in which the dreamer goes back to an earlier stage of his existence, are far more common in the dreams of adolescents and adults. The dreams in the Infants' schools having been collected at the end of November and during December, accounts for so many prospective dreams of Christmas. In their dreams the actual presents are described in detail. The doll with the inevitable doll's pram bulks largely in the young girl's dream. Even up to the age of nine years, the wish for the "pram" is definitely mentioned with the doll in 90 per cent. of the dreams of this type.

The fact that very young children dream far less about food than the older children indicates that they are the last to suffer in the case of food shortage in the home.   The dream is a sure indication of the position of the child in this respect, as is clearly shown by a comparison of the proportion of food dreams among children in poor and well-to-do districts.   The child who dreams frequently about food may reasonably be assumed to be an underfed child.   A striking case is recorded of the value of the dream in this connection.   A well-known investigator was carrying on a research on the physiological effects of a short period of starvation.   He remained without food for six days, and after the first day was not conscious of any personal inconvenience, but every night he dreamed of having hearty meals though he had never experienced this type of dream before.   On resuming his normal life, the food dreams ceased.

The association of the disappearance of the ghost with the advent of the fairy story is supported by evidence of the dreams of older children.   There is a tendency for the ghost to reappear when the interest in the fairy story ceases, and it is much more common in boys' than in girls' dreams. Other reasons for the disappearance are the general decline of a belief in ghosts, and the decrease in the amount of ghost-story literature.

The state of health of the child has an important influence on the dream. During any complaint which involves raising of the normal temperature, dreams become much more frequent, there being often three or four in one night. The dream alters in type, and becomes increasingly vivid, and not infrequently the death element enters. The dream now conforms more closely to the neurotic type, but becomes normal again on the child's restoration to health.

In the Infants' school, the careful study of dreams may yield very valuable results in giving additional information as to the actual normal temperament of the child, its unfulfilled wishes, its state of health, and in children of the neurotic type, it may give important clues to the basis of the mental instability. With monthly records extending over a year, the persistent elements in the dream could be separated from the waking elements, and this would give a valuable insight into the unconscious make-up of the child.

CHAPTER IV

DREAMS OF CHILDREN OF EIGHT TO
FOURTEEN YEARS OF AGE

THE large number of dreams of children in the elementary schools available for examination makes the results more reliable than those in other schools in which there was less material for investigation. In the industrial, blind and deaf, central and secondary schools, there is naturally an overlap of children of the same range of age, and in dealing with the dreams of pupils in these schools in order to avoid unnecessary repetition in the details of the analyses, reference will only be made to points of difference compared with the results obtained in the normal elementary schools, and to any special features observed in the dreams of children of more advanced age.

48

Analysis of Dream Elements of Boys and Girls in the Normal Elementary Schools

Fulfilled Wishes.—The number of clearly expressed fulfilled wishes differs considerably in boys' and girls' dreams, the percentage varying from about 28 per cent. in the case of boys, to 42 per cent. in the case of girls. The nature of the wishes also varies. The girl dreams far more about the return of father and relatives from the war ; about presents of various kinds ; about eating, and above all, about visits to the country, travelling, and entertainments. On the other hand, boys have six times as many dreams about bravery and adventure as the girls, and these might reasonably be included among the wish-fulfillment dreams. At the age of thirteen, there is a marked increase in this type of dream among the girls.

The eating element in dreams falls off after the age of ten, and presents, other than food, decrease after this age, whereas the dreams of visits to the country tend to increase. Dreams of presents and eating, at all ages from nine to fourteen, are much more common with children from the poorer than from the well-to-do districts.

The majority of the dreams recorded being

D

at the end of November, and the early part of December, there were many prospective dreams of Christmas, especially among the girls of eight and nine years of age. There is a great falling off in this type of dream after ten years of age, and this is common to both boys' and girls' dreams. Retrospective dreams among young children are very uncommon.

Fear Dreams.—Boys have more fear dreams (19 per cent.) than girls (16 per cent.). The most marked difference is in the fear of burglars and robbers, which appears twice as often in boys' as in girls' dreams. Girls dream rather more of strange men and women than boys, but the difference is not marked. It is the old man who is the terror of the dreaming boy and girl. He is responsible in both cases for about half the fear dreams. The fear of animals is practically the same in both sexes, and is the cause of about 20 per cent. of fear dreams. The larger animals, *e.g.*, lions, tigers, and bulls, predominate in boys', and dogs, rats, mice and snakes in girls' dreams. The ghost has practically disappeared from the child's dream, but occurs occasionally when the fairy-story dream begins to wane. It is more common in boys' than in girls' dreams. Dreams of the house being on fire affect the

boy equally with the girl : rather less than
10 per cent. of fear dreams are of this
nature.

Kinæsthetic Dreams.—Among these are
included falling dreams, loss of muscular
control in movement and speech, and
dreams in which excessive movement is the
predominating element. Dreams of this
type only occur occasionally among children
of eight-and nine years of age, and at these
ages much more frequently among boys than
girls. It is at the age of ten that they form
an important element in children's dreams,
and from that age to fourteen they increase
steadily. Boys have more kinæsthetic
dreams than girls, the proportion being ten to
seven. The gliding, floating and swimming
elements are more common among girls, and
the falling element among boys. The unmis-
takable appearance of this type of dream as
an important factor at the age of ten deserves
full investigation. It would appear, from the
analysis of dream elements, that the well-to-
do child is more subject to this kind of dream
than the poorer child, and this is strength-
ened by the results obtained by examination
of the dreams of children in secondary and
industrial schools.

Pleasurable Dreams about Animals.—
Dreams of this nature are common among

young children, especially boys of eight to nine years of age. They rarely occur after the age of ten.

School Activities.—Although the normal child spends nearly half the day in, or associated with, the school, it is remarkable that so few dreams have any direct reference to the school ; and where this is the case, the reference is rather to the activities of the playground and swimming-bath than of the classroom. The girls' dreams are more influenced by school activities than the boys', but the number is almost negligible. There is not the slightest evidence of worry or overstrain in this connection even in the classroom dream. Rehearsals and performances of plays are occasional elements in dreams, and the striking success of the dreamer in his or her part is not infrequently a source of gratification. Indirectly, the school has a great influence on the dream. The fairy story has a very marked effect. The teacher, moreover, especially in girls' dreams, figures very prominently in dreams of many out-of-school experiences.

Air Raids.—Most of the accounts of the dreams were written six months after the last air raid was experienced in London. It is interesting to observe that, especially among the children of eight and nine years of age, the memory of the air raid has practically ceased to trouble the dreamer. Among the older children dreams of raids, especially girls' dreams, appear to be more in evidence, but they are generally vivid dreams, not of recent date.

One set of dreams from a girls' school was written two months before the others, and these were markedly influenced by the air raids.

Bravery and Adventure.—Here there is a very marked difference between boys' and girls' dreams. The war had a much greater effect on the boys than on the girls. Even at the age of eight, boys dream of performing heroic deeds ; at nine years of age, the number of dreams containing these elements increases, and continues to increase to the end of the elementary school period. A large proportion of the dream elements of the boy are of this nature. The dreamers are often mentioned in despatches, win the Victoria Cross, are personally thanked by the King, and, on returning home from the war, are cheered by grateful crowds. Girls' dreams of bravery and adventure do not occur before the age of ten, and the number of such dreams is insignificant until the age of thirteen, when there is a decided change, and deeds of valour generally as Red Cross nurses on the battlefield are not infrequent. The total number of boys' dreams involving deeds of valour compared with girls' is as six to one.

Cinema and Book Dreams.—Whatever may be the indirect influence of the cinema on the dreaming child, only a relatively small number of dreams appear to be directly affected, and this occurs chiefly among the older boys. The number of girls' dreams directly influenced is insignificant. The book read just before going to bed affects the dreamer, and is often referred to by an explanatory note following the record of a strange dream, in which the child takes the part of one of the leading characters. Similar explanations are also sometimes given of what are evidently cinema dreams.

Fairy Stories.—The influence of fairy stories on the dreamer, especially the girl dreamer, is very marked. Greatest at eight years of age, it has a considerable effect throughout the school period. Generally, the dream of this type is of the most pleasurable nature. The number of girls' dreams influenced by fairy stories is four times as great as in the case of boys. Above the age of ten the fairy story ceases to have much effect on the boys' dreams.

Dreams in which the Child is not present.— A few dreams are recorded—principally those of boys—in which incidents of the war are vividly described, in which the dreamer was not present.   They generally refer to events affecting the welfare of relatives, and many presentiments of the loss of friends obtained in this way are said by the dreamers to have come true.

Dreams   with   Conversation.— Definitely recorded   conversations   are   common   in children's dreams, and they are rather more frequent in girls' than in boys' dreams.   At eight years of age they are comparatively rare, and at ten reach the maximum ; then, in boys' dreams, they decrease in number at subsequent ages, whereas among girls the maximum is reached at the same age, but the proportion is practically retained until the end of the school period.

The   Death   Element.—Dreams in which the interest centres around the death of the dreamer or of some friend are not uncommon, even among children of eight years of age. Rarely the older child dreams that he is present at his own funeral as a spectator, and describes the scene.

The Presence of Members of the Family Group and Friends in the Dream.—In the dream of the very young child, the dreamer is generally the only witness of the dream; later, the mother is often present, and at eight or nine years of age, other members of the family and sometimes school-mates take part. At ten and eleven years of age, the boy's chum and the particular friend of the girl, practically always of the same sex as the dreamer, tend to replace members of the family group; and at subsequent ages, the dreamer alone, or the dreamer and friend are generally the central figures. The proportion of dreams in which the friend or friends of the dreamer takes an active part is fairly constant, both in boys' and girls' dreams throughout the school period.

Love Sentiment.—Anything in the nature of sentiment between members of the opposite sex is very rarely found in the dreams of children from eight to fourteen years of age, but is more common in girls' than in boys' dreams.

From such a large number of dreams, it is very difficult to make a selection to illustrate even a small number of the many points which have arisen during the course of the investigation. It will be noticed that in the records of dreams of young children there is a considerable amount of secondary elaboration, and the omission of gaps in the dream material and incidents contrary to experience in order to secure a connected narrative.

The following dreams are fairly typical. The age and sex of the dreamer is stated in each case.

DOMESTIC DREAMS

(a) *A boy of* 8 :

I can not tell you my dream last night, but I can tell you my other dream the night before. I dreamt that I was going to be washed. And then I was being put in the bath to be washed. After I was washed, I was wrung out in the mangle. Then I was hung on the line. I was hanging on the line when it started to rain. My mother took me in and ironed me. The iron was hot. And then I woke up.

(b) *A girl of* 8 :

On last Friday, I dreamt I was out in a wood with some other girls. As we were in the wood we heard the robin as he hopped from branch to branch singing and chirping all the time. We went on till one of them said there's a wood-nut tree. Come and look for nuts. So then away we ran to pick up the nuts which had fallen down. I thought I had filled up all my pockets with them. Soon we were getting tired, so we had a nice meal of tomato sandwiches and then a glass of lemonade to cool us. Of course we kept picking flowers. The air seemed sweet the white and blue sky was above us, and birds singing up in the trees, and everything seemed bright and happy. In the morning, I felt disappointed about the nuts, and I wish this dream was at day time instead of night time, then I should enjoy it much better.

(c) *A girl of* 8 :

I dreamt I was married and had a little girl at school, also I had a little baby. My husband was a soldier in France. My girl had long curly hair. She wore a white frock with a blue sash and white shoes and stockings. But one night as I got into bed I heard the maroons go off. My children were fast asleep, so I got the eldest up first. I dressed them, and put their hats and coats on and then dressed myself. Then I ran down the tube. A little while after I heard it was all clear, and when I got home I had just put my children to bed, when I heard a rat-tat. I went and opened the door, and my husband walked in. He was home on leave. He was an officer. I was a school teacher. I had the first class, and a little while after I joined the "Wax." When I woke up, I found it was only a dream.

FAIRY-STORY DREAM

A girl of 8 :

Last night I dreamt that I was in Fairy Land, and that I had beautiful little fairies to wait upon me. One day, a little fairy said to me, "Would you like to come into the wood with us?" and so I said "Yes." So we went into the wood, and we saw lots of rabbits running about. Presently the fairies thought it was time to go home, so we went home and had tea. For tea we had ice cakes and cream. Then we went out and had some moonbeam slides like all fairies like to do. Soon after we went home to bed. Now our beds were not made of iron, they were made of moss with rose petals for pillows and fern leaves for a cover. Just as I was going to sleep, I awoke.

FEAR DREAMS

(*a*) *A girl of* 9 :

The dream I dreamt last night was impossible. I was going in the grocer's when I noticed that the owner of the shop instead of sprinkling sawdust on the floor he sprinkled sugar, and of course I trod on it. Then he sent for the policeman, and told him that I had trodden on his precious sugar, and then I was taken to the police station. The next day I was to have my trial. When I was in the court, I was very frightened. Much to my sorrow, my sentence was that I should be hung in three days. On the fourth day, I was very sad because this was my last hour. Presently, I heard soldiers unlocking the door of my cell. Then sadly I walked to the scaffold. But directly my feet touched the scaffold I awoke.

(b) *A boy of* 11 :

I dreamt that I was lost in one of the busy parts of London. I was walking towards a policeman to enquire of my whereabouts, when I became suddenly surrounded by vehicles of all sorts. By dodging between them, I at last reached the policeman who told me I was in Fleet Street. The rolls of paper which I saw afterwards, confirmed his statement. I went into a tube station, and asked the booking clerk if there were trains to Kennington, as I had enough money for the fare. The booking clerk answered in the affirmative, and I travelled as far as the Oval by train and walked the rest of the way home.   I then awoke.

BRAVERY AND ADVENTURE

(*a*) *A boy of* 10 :

I dreamt I was out for a walk in Hyde Park and as I was walking down the Row, I saw a man walking across it, while a horse thundered down upon him.   At once I could see that the poor man was blind, so I did not hesitate, but rushed out under the rails to try and save the man.   Acting under the impulse of the moment, I shouted to the rider of the horse, who tried in vain to stop the animal, which still rushed on, so I caught hold of the blind man and dragged him to safety.   How surprised I was, when I found I had saved one of the millionaires.   He overwhelmed me with thanks and invited me to dinner next day, where his wife and children nearly smothered me with thanks.   After dinner was over, and we had a little chat, it was time for me to go, he gave me an envelope which he told me not to open till I got home.   When I was alone, I opened it, and found a cheque for a million pounds inside. So ended my dream, which unfortunately was not true, for I heard the alarm clock ringing, so I knew that it was a dream. But after all it had a happy ending, which some dreams have not, but mine had.

(b) *A boy of* 10 :

I dreamt that I was a soldier, and as I was in a trench a lot of Huns jumped in and took me prisoner. I was taken to a castle, and as I was in a dungeon the Kaiser and his son William went past the door. I escaped, and searched about till I found a room. I looked in and saw the Kaiser talking to Hindenburg, I crept in and wrote down all they said, and as a German soldier went past, I jumped on him and killed him, and took his bayonet and crept back. Hindenburg was not there, so I jumped on the Kaiser and killed him with the bayonet. Just as I was creeping out, I woke up on the floor.

(c) *A girl of* 12 :

I dreamt I was elected M.P. for Fulham. Lloyd George decided to send me out to Germany to try and persuade the Kaiser to give up fighting. I do not know how I got to Germany. I was suddenly there. The Kaiser took a fancy to me, and I lived at his palace, and was educated with his children.   There were four girls and three boys, and they all dressed in brown holland. There were two other children living with us, a small French boy and an English girl.   One day the Kaiser took us for a drive in his motor, and as we were going up a very steep hill, I asked the Kaiser to give up fighting.   He was so amazed that he let go of the steering-wheel, and the car slid backwards down the hill and shot us through the palace windows into the dancing hall where the dancing mistress was waiting to give a lesson.   Presently the Kaiser called us and told us that he must fly into Holland and that the German fleet was going to surrender.   I then escaped in a submarine, and woke up when it bumped against the shores of England.

The Death Element

A girl of 13:

Last night I had a most peculiar dream, part of which I cannot recall.   At first I saw my brother in naval uniform on a ship. I then saw my mother crying, and then I seemed to be gazing into nothingness. Previous to this period I was standing beside my teacher having my sums marked. Again I saw my brother, then slowly he faded away, and all seemed in a confusion. Gradually my mother came into sight, and then a military funeral. The coffin which I dreamt bore my brother, was covered with a Union Jack and crowned with flowers. This was not all; beside me in full uniform stood my brother, who was viewing his own funeral. Then came the conclusion, I saw my mother weeping, then everything faded away, and, when I awoke, I discovered my pillow was wet with tears.

KINÆSTHETIC DREAMS

(a) *A boy of* 12 :

I was fishing by a river in the country when I saw a young boy fall in the river. Although I could not swim, I jumped in after him. It was rather deep, but somehow I reached the boy. After having reached the boy, everything seemed to fade away. But strange to say, the next instant I found myself on a swift travelling boat, and by my side was the boy I had rescued. Somehow I found out that I was on a fire-boat. The thing that pleased me most was that the boat was going to a fire. Then I saw that the boat was going to my own house. Oh! how frightened I felt. Then, all of a sudden, I seemed to be in my bed, shouting out "Grandad! the bed's on fire!" Next I seemed to be first burning hot and then ever so cold. Then, in through my window a spurt of water from the hose came all over me. Once more I seemed not to be in bed but on the fire-boat, and in my hands was a hose. There I stood, squirting water into my ᵥown bedroom. Then all seemed to get muddled up, and I awoke to see the rain coming in the window, and on to me. Somehow I felt glad that that dream was over, and somehow I seemed to enjoy it.

(*b*) *A boy of* 12 :

One night I went to bed very late, and I had a nice dream. I dreamt I was flying along the sky with some birds and we flew on a mountain top. On the top of the mountain was a big nest as big as a haystack, there were other younger birds in the nest, and they were pleased to see me. The next morning, I had a good breakfast of boiled eggs and mutton, after breakfast, all the little birds flew on another mountain top which afterwards they told me was their school. Then they came back with

E

two fat calves and a basket of eggs which they robbed. The mother bird cooked some eggs for me and fried some meat, which I enjoyed. After dinner we slept. I was soon awake at tea time, but instead of tea I had milk, but the birds had water. Then the mother bird took me to a little room where there was a cosy bed. I was soon asleep, but I was awakened by my mother, who said it was time to get up.

(c) *A girl of* 13 :

The last dream I had was not very pleasant. I was walking along when I saw a little girl. I asked her if she would come for a walk with me. She said she would be pleased to come. While we were walking along, in front of us stood a high wall, which we tried to climb, and as we got near the top, so we fell down again. I tried to speak to the little girl, but I found she had gone, and I was alone, so I went and turned back, and I found myself on the top of Nelson's monument, and all at once all the four lions came and lay at my feet. I looked at all the people, and they all called to me to come down. I tried to jump, and I found myself in bed.

PROSPECTIVE DREAMS (Christmas)

(a) *A boy of* 12 :

Yesterday while I was sleeping in bed, I suddenly found that I was walking down the stairs of my house into the kitchen. I walked slowly into the kitchen, where to my surprise, I saw a large table covered with delicious eatables, such as Christmas pudding and turkey and meat. I went upstairs and in my bedroom instead of a bed there stood another large table covered with a snow white cloth, and in the centre was a pudding with holly stuck in it. I went to cut a piece off for myself, and to my disappointment I found it had vanished, so I had to go without. Many children sat round the table and of course every one wanted something to eat. Soon as they had finished one pudding I gave them another. All the walls were hung with holly and Christmas chains. All the children were enjoying themselves very much all except me, who was not having anything to eat. I tried to take something off the dishes but everything disappeared from my sight. I went downstairs to find my mother but she was nowhere to be found. I searched everywhere but I could not find her.. I suddenly slipped over a piece of orange peel and bumped my head against a table and then I woke up to find I had been dreaming in bed all the time, which made me very disappointed.

(*b*) *A girl of* 12 :

I dreamt that my mother bought me and my sister a large Christmas tree, and on this tree there was a number of tiny little candles which were of different colours, and there was a lot of toys hanging on it. Mother had a wish-bone, which she had kept and she said that we could see who got the wish and so we pulled and I had the wish. I wished that my Dad was home on Christmas day. When Christmas day came we were dressed in our best, and our uncles and aunts had come and we were enjoying ourselves. We went into the parlour and we found somebody dressed up as Santa Claus, and he asked us what we wanted off the tree. When we had got what we wanted he took off the clothes of Santa Claus and it was my father and so my wish came true, and then I woke up and told mother.

DREAMS WITH CONVERSATION

(*a*) *A girl of* 12 :

On Sunday night I dreamt that I was

walking through a thick forest, where upon I met a lion who looked very fierce. He was very faithful to me, he licked me and made such a fuss of me that I did not feel frightened a bit. But presently I saw my mother coming in the distance who told me to come home, my mother said : "What business have you to come into this forest?" I was crying because my mother spoke very sternly, so I said to my mother, "Mother, may I have a little talk with my friend?" My mother said : "No, come home to tea." So I said good-bye to my friend, then I woke up.

(*b*) *A girl of* 13 :

I dreamt that I was sitting by the fire wishing to be with my aunt, when I heard a noise that sounded like somebody patting the window. I went forward and opened it and into the room a little white mouse jumped. After giving it some milk it seemed to grow bigger and when it had grown as big as Beal, my kitten, he said to me, " Every egg that you have eaten, has made you a bigger criminal." At this I was very astonished and said, "Why?" " Because you have eaten a great number of chickens." "They are very little use," I answered, and with this I went out of the room.

DREAM AT WHICH DREAMER NOT PRESENT

A girl of 13:

I dreamt that we had a dog named Jack who loved his master very much, and after Daddy had been out in France for a little while the dog found its way to France and then found Daddy. He was ever so surprised at seeing the dog, and asked the general if he might take it home, and he was given permission to do so, and that was how we got Daddy home in my dream. Then soon after I woke up.

The following is a particularly interesting dream, or rather series of three dreams, which were dreamt in the same night by a girl of twelve years of age. In each part the kinæsthetic element predominates. The rapid transition from one type of experience to another is very striking and assumes rather the form of a continuous nightmare than a normal dream. For convenience, I divide it into three sections.

1st Section.—At the beginning I found myself in the house next door, with a lot of horrid men running after me, and when they caught me they said they were going to kill me, so I was put out between two lions and in ten minutes a huge wave was coming up the road and it came right over me.   Then I heard some clapping and I had just finished singing a song before all the school.

2nd Section.—I was in my own bedroom and there was a lion under my bed and in the cupboard was a terrible ghost.   I heard him walking about and then he came out and ran after me and I was on a bicycle riding round the bed with the ghost after me.   All at once I jumped out of the window with a great scream then I woke up and found myself on the floor.

3rd Section.—I went to sleep again and dreamt that Mother and Father had turned into cabbages and I was getting them ready for dinner but just as I was putting them into the saucepan they turned into people again, and asked me if I liked the aeroplane which we were in, and then I found myself in a Handley-Page.   I was driving it when all of a sudden it vanished and I was swimming in the sea.   When I woke up I was sitting up in bed, and it was morning so I did not dream any more that night.

Girls of twelve and thirteen dream much about religion, and there were several interest-

ing dreams of heaven.   Even in these there
is a curious, almost ludicrous, admixture of
everyday experiences.

One girl after describing the scene adds :
" Much information was given to us (girl and
friend) by a nice gentleman who, I presume,
was a cherub.   In appearance he strongly
reminded me of our school caretaker."
Another, after describing the kindness of the
angels to herself and her friend, concludes :
" We had tea with them and they afterwards
kindly assisted us in the washing-up."

The rapid change from one kind of experience to another of an entirely different order
is well shown in the dream of a girl of twelve.
She is trying to rescue a drowning girl and
meets one of her teachers in the water, who
tells her that she must hurry to school at once
because " governess wants you to take the
part of Julius Cæsar."

In the dreams of bravery and adventure
the boys show a considerable knowledge of
the technical details of warfare, but the girls
give no evidence of it.   A girl of fourteen
states : " I found myself in Germany with my
friend, Margaret, telling the Germans to hold

up their arms while we shot them.   I dreamt we killed every German soldier in the land." Girls who ride in aeroplanes generally land successfully, but the boys nearly always crash.

A curious case of the reversal of experience is given in the case of a boy of twelve, who dreamt that he was chased by Christmas puddings with knives and forks stuck in them, and woke up just as they were going to eat him.

Children often combine in their dreams the incidents of the day before, bringing them to a happy conclusion.   As one girl states : " I generally dream of doing something I could not do the day before."   There is much evidence in the dreams of the clearing up of difficult situations.

Jealousy of other girls comes into girls' dreams at about the age of fourteen.   At this age the girl friend is very prominent in the dream.   Jealousy does not enter into the boy's dream.

Boys dream far more about sports than girls.   In the dream records girls describe the scene in more detail than the boys, and include descriptions of the attire of the chief participants.

Children of twelve and thirteen appear to dream much less than younger and older children, and some of the dreams have a morbid tendency.

At eleven years of age there are many cases of people changing into animals and vice versa. The head mistress becomes a horse, an old man becomes a mauve cow with green eyes, the brother of a girl of this age changes into a dog, goes to school as usual and she rides home on his back. Rapid alterations in the size of objects in dreams appear to occur more frequently at the ages of thirteen and fourteen than at others.

The comparative absence of references to school activities is referred to above in the analysis of dream elements. There is a distinct fun element in the following dream of a girl of twelve: " I dreamt that we were having an English lesson. Miss —— was taking us and we came across the word legs. We were such dunces that we did not know what legs meant so Miss —— showed us her

legs.   I was sitting next to Lucy —— and
we started to laugh.   Then Miss —— told us
not to be so rude."

During the war the Food Controller had
practically no effect upon the dreams of the
children.   Rations were only mentioned four
times in the whole of the dreams.   The
prominence of the aunt in the child's dream
up to the age of twelve is very striking.   She
is a veritable good fairy, and a large proportion of the wish-fulfilment dreams are
associated with her in one way or another.
She figures in very many dreams of both
boys and girls, and is invariably a good kind
person evidently much loved by the dreamers.

CHAPTER V

DREAMS OF CHILDREN OF FOURTEEN TO EIGHTEEN YEARS OF AGE

THE dreams dealt with in this chapter consist mainly of those of girls from secondary schools in which the range of age is ten to eighteen years ; the others are dreams of boys and girls in central schools in which the age of the dreamer varies from ten to fifteen or sixteen years.   In the latter the dreams of children of the same age as those in the normal school present very few points of difference and need not be further considered. In those above the age of fourteen the most striking changes are the following :—

(1) A great falling off in the proportion of fear dreams among the boys, whereas among the girls the proportion is maintained. In the latter the fear of strange men and women increases.

(2) A considerable increase in both boys and girls of the number of kinæsthetic dreams.

(3) An increase in the death element dreams among the girls and a marked decrease among the boys.

(4) Many more references to the school activities in the dreams of both boys and girls.

(5) A further increase in the proportion of dreams of bravery and adventure among the boys, but no apparent increase among the girls.

(6) In both boys' and girls' dreams the influence of fairy stories has practically disappeared.

There are many interesting points of difference between the dreams of girls of the same age in secondary and those in elementary schools, and considerable changes occur in the nature of the dreams of the older girls.

COMPARISON OF DREAMS OF GIRLS IN SECONDARY SCHOOLS WITH THOSE IN ELEMENTARY SCHOOLS

In making this comparison it must be borne in mind that the range of age in secondary schools is ten to eighteen years, whereas in elementary schools the range is eight to fourteen years.

Taking first the ten to fourteen period common to both types of schools, some striking differences are to be noted :—

(1) The total number of fulfilled wishes in the dreams of the secondary school girl is very much reduced, especially those of presents other than food, and dreams about eating. In the latter, meals are rarely mentioned, the eating dreams referring rather to presents of sweets or chocolates. On the other hand, the number of fulfilled wishes referring to visits to the country, travelling, and parties, largely exceed those in elementary schools.

(2) Fear dreams are rather more common among girls in secondary schools than among those in elementary schools, especially those connected with strange men and women. Dreams of ghosts are more frequent, and there is greater fear of animals.

(3) The proportion of kinæsthetic dreams is very much greater among the secondary than the elementary school girls, especially at eleven and twelve years of age.

(4) At all ages the secondary school girl dreams more about school activities than the elementary school girl. The fact that so many of the former type remain at school for the mid-day interval is an important factor. This results in the formation of more enduring friendships. In residential girls' schools this is still more accentuated.

(5) Cinema films and the reading of exciting books before going to bed have more effect on the dreams of girls in secondary schools than on those in elementary schools.

(6) The fairy story up to the age of fourteen affects the dreams of the secondary school girl as much as those of the elementary school girl.

The most important changes in the content of the dreams of the secondary school girl above the elementary school age are the following :—

(1) There is a steady decrease in the fulfilled wishes about relatives coming home from the war, presents of any kind, and dreams about eating ; but there is an increase in the proportion of those dealing with other

forms of enjoyment. The material nature of the fulfilled wishes tends to disappear.

(2) There is a striking increase found at the age of sixteen in the proportion of fear dreams, especially those connected with animals and strange men and women.

(3) There is little change in the proportion of kinæsthetic dreams from twelve to fifteen years of age, but a further increase is to be observed at sixteen and seventeen years. For the whole range of the secondary school the proportion of kinæsthetic dreams is twice that of the elementary school, but it should be remembered that up to the age of ten this type of dream is comparatively rare.

(4) From fourteen to seventeen years of age the girl dreams far more of her school activities than during the early years of the secondary school.

(5) Above the age of fourteen the cinema and exciting book and the fairy story appear to have little effect on the girls' dreams.

(6) The conversation in the dream, which is a common element in about 10 per cent. of girls' dreams up to fourteen years of age, is rarely found in those of older girls.

(7) At fourteen years of age there is an increase in the number of dreams in which

the death element occurs. After that the proportion again becomes normal.

(8) Love sentiment dreams are more common at fifteen than at any other age of the secondary school period.

The following are a few typical dreams :—

DOMESTIC DREAM

A girl of 15 :

I was seated in a boot shop, which somehow seemed something like our kitchen, and yet it had all the fittings of a shop where new boots were sold, and others mended. My father and mother were both there, and I was asking to see some fancy indoor shoes.

The first pair the man brought me were of black glace kid, with patent leather toe-caps and high heels. They were similar to what are called court shoes, having no straps. I put them on and they fitted me perfectly, so I asked the price of them, and was very much astonished to hear that they were five pounds four and six-pence. I told the shop-keeper that they were too much, and inquired if he had something a little cheaper. He then brought a pair of rather shabby black brocaded ones, also with high heels.

F

These also fitted me, and again I asked the price, which went to the opposite extreme, for they were only twopence halfpenny.

I do not know whether I had these or not, for my dream suddenly ended, but I remember that both pairs had rubber heels, and I distinctly heard my father say that one of the pairs was to have the rubber taken off and a piece of leather put on instead.

This dream almost seemed real, it was so vivid. I can even remember that one of the black brocade shoes had a tiny darn on one toe.

It seems that I am bound to dream of shoes this week, for last night I was the proud owner of a pair of blue satin ball shoes, ornamented with diamonds. One shoe was mended slightly for me, and then I put them on and walked about as proud as a peacock. Everybody had to admire them and I even walked out in the street with them on.

Bravery and Adventure

A girl of 14 :

I dreamt that I was captured by a German. I was sent to the palace of the

Kaiser, as it was a very unusual occurrence for a girl to be captured. On arriv-
ing there I was taken to the Kaiserin.
She received me very kindly. I was then
taken to the Kaiser, who gave me a pen,
and told me to sign a paper ; as this paper
was printed in German, I asked him what
it meant, but he told me to do as I was
told.

After signing the paper, the Kaiserin
gave me something to eat. She was very
kind to me, so I said, "I thought that
Germans were horrid people, but you have
been very kind to me." To this she re-
plied, "Yes, some are nice and some are
not."

I told her that I had learnt a little
German in school, and she seemed very
pleased.

After a time I saw something about a
post office ; I mentioned this to her, and
she said, "Yes, that is what I intend
putting you into, but of course your
earnings will come to me, because you
must remember you are only a prisoner."

The Kaiserin told me that she would
befriend me, but would not let the Kaiser
know.

When the Kaiser fled they went in a
carriage. I was to have gone in the car-

riage too, but I thought it too great an honour, and so I rode on the back.

We stayed for a night at an inn, but as I was a prisoner, I slept in the stables. When we arrived in Holland the Kaiserin gave me in charge of a homely family, who were to send me back to England. When I said good-bye the Kaiserin slipped some notes into my hand, to pay for my homeward journey.

School Activities

(a) *A girl of* 14:

Last Thursday I went to bed thinking of nothing but the dreadful to-morrow. It was our Latin examination! It is not that I do not like Latin; on the contrary, I am very fond of it, but when I thought of the awful exam. looming ahead, I felt as if I did not know anything at all. The next thing I remember was seeing my fatal red Latin book open and out of its leaves sprang innumerable little men; they did not look like anything I had ever seen before; they were pixies.

The only thing my pixies seemed to do was to frisk about in a most bewildering fashion, but at last I understood; they were my Latin declensions. After a little while they were all arranged in a neat and trim order, and there was my Latin book.

But, alas! just as I was getting on so beautifully with my unexpected Latin revision, at a sudden sharp order from the pronoun "hic" all my pixies jumped up into the air, and I awoke to the plain fact that it was Friday and the dreaded day had arrived.

(*b*) *A girl of* 16 :

There was nobody to be seen in or near the school and the whole place looked a deserted ruin. I took the cloakroom key and unlocked the cloakroom for myself and came to the form-room. All over the floor there were piles of books which looked old and torn. As I opened the door they all jumped up and asked me what I wanted there ; and a history book asked me if I was Oliver Cromwell and a geography book asked me from what country I came, and whether the climate was a Mediterranean one or not ; while a grammar book looked reproachfully at me and said, "Why do you dislike me so?" I fled from the room with the books following me all round the school!

DREAM WITH CONVERSATION

A girl of 12 :

I had the following dream on the night of 10th November, the night before the "Cease Fire" Armistice was signed.

The Kaiser and his chancellors were seated at a long table, debating whether to sign the armistice or not. The Kaiser sat twirling his moustache angrily. He glanced round the table at the assembled people. Suddenly a flash of lightning lit up the room, then almost at the same time a terrific crash of thunder burst upon them. The Kaiser went pale. Then his favourite Chancellor spoke : " The delay will do no good ; sign it, Sire." The Kaiser glanced at his friend, picked up his pen and signed the armistice. The wind outside stopped, the rain ceased and through the clouds floated a white figure, with a shining crown, and on it was written " Peace." It floated through the open window, hovered over the assembled company and disappeared. The sun came out and shone on the Kaiser and his men.

The Kaiser stood up ; " The audience is at an end," he said. The Chancellors stood up and silently walked out, leaving the Kaiser to his meditations.

Then I awoke.

DEATH ELEMENT

A girl of 13 :

I dreamt that I was ill and had several doctors in attendance. The doctors said that I was dying and could not live more than a few hours, while I felt that I was rapidly recovering. This I told the doctors, and no sooner had I said it than they began to do all manner of things to make me die sooner. They were very funny ways of killing people ; one was this—one of the doctors put a doctor's thermometer in my mouth and began to heat the mercury in the bulb saying that as the mercury rose up the thermometer I should feel as if I was having gas administered to me at the dentists and gradually get more drowsy and yet more drowsy until I should drop off to sleep and never wake again. But this did not succeed, for instead of getting drowsy I felt more awake than was usual. Then the doctor told mother to throw the window right up because fresh air would kill anyone, and mother was actually so hard-hearted as to do it. But, of course, this did not kill but only revived me. Then the doctors all lost their tempers and said that they did not care whether I lived or died and left me alone. Then I began to get well quickly, but mother felt sure that I was dying and insisted on my saying farewell to everyone in the house, and just as I was saying good-bye to my baby brother I awoke—screaming with fright.

KINÆSTHETIC DREAM

A girl of 13 :

I suddenly had a feeling of going downwards with a regular movement. I thought I was going down to a tube station in a lift, but somebody seemed to be saying, "Nearly through water, nearly through the water." A few seconds later the moving stopped and I got out. A man, with one leg, who said he was a discharged soldier, told me that I was under the English Channel waiting for a vehicle, which was suspended in the water, to take me round the world in half an hour.

These vehicles were worked entirely by discharged soldiers, who had been trying for some time to bring them to perfection.

I found this mode of travelling had several disadvantages, for it was far below the sea, and there was no view, so that you could see nothing of the countries under which you were passing. Another disadvantage was that it had no stops, and there was no point in going round the world, only to return home half an hour later.

While I was thus travelling, I think I must have gone into a sounder sleep, for I never remember coming to the surface again.

The dreams quoted above of children below the age of fourteen are those of girls from secondary schools.

A girl of sixteen records three dreams she had in one week. The kinæsthetic element is common to all of them.

I have marked the dreams (*a*) (*b*) and (*c*).

A girl of 16 :

(*a*) I was standing at the top of a huge precipice. Below me, deep down, a mighty river could be seen. The sun could not reach down. I leaned farther over the edge. The sides of the precipice were covered with ferns and flowers. A bright flower down below me made me desire to pick it. I stretched out my hand and sank down, down, down. It seemed I would never reach the bottom. Suddenly I struck something and—I was awake.

(*b*) I was in Antwerp. German soldiers could be seen drilling in our tiny street. I could not speak Flemish and the Belgians could not speak English. I determined to get away from our hateful oppressors. It was four o'clock on a cold, misty morning when I disappeared from Antwerp. I reached the country outside the town and walked, unknowingly, into a group of soldiers. They asked me why it was that I was outside the town at that time. They spoke to me in English, but they were Germans. I appeared not to understand, and, as they were drunk, I soon escaped from them. All I knew after this was that I walked a long, long way until I had reached safety.

(*c*) Something was behind me; I was running as if I had wings. After some time I felt all the power go out of me, and I stood quite still—and nothing happened. I turned round but could see nothing because it was dark. The stillness oppressed me. I wanted to run. Again I started to run, and again I felt I was pursued by something. Each time I stopped the mysterious pursuer stopped. Home appeared in front of me. But everything seemed set out to trip me up. Things then seemed to turn upside down.

When I had reached home something rushed past the window and I was safe!

From a preface to a dream of a girl of fifteen it appeared that she was in great trouble at having to leave her school and go to a college for a course of special training. She was also distressed because her father had refused to give her a bicycle. The dream that followed was a typical wish-fulfilment dream.

At her first appearance at the College she found that many of her old friends from school were there, and after the happiest of days she rode home on a bicycle which her father had given to her.

With girls of fourteen and fifteen dreams of great friendships and violent quarrels with other girls of the same school are not infrequent.

The chief pleasure dreams of girls of fifteen to seventeen are of the seaside, and bathing is the central element.

From thirteen years of age onwards a few of the girls' dreams become more difficult to resolve into simple elements, and this difficulty becomes more accentuated in the dreams of girls of sixteen, seventeen and eighteen. In these there appears to be a certain amount of camouflage which only the psycho-analytic expert could deal with effectively.

CHAPTER VI

DREAMS OF CHILDREN IN INDUSTRIAL SCHOOLS

THE dreams of children in industrial schools are of special interest, and in some respects they have marked characteristics which separate them clearly from those of normal elementary school children. The dreams are frequent and vivid. The age range is ten to sixteen years. There is nothing to indicate harsh treatment at the schools, and the fact that many of the teachers play a friendly part in the dreams, coming to the rescue in perilous times, and in many other ways, shows that the children are on good terms with those in authority. The comparative monotony of institutional life, however, finds undoubted solace in the dreams of fulfilled wishes and those of bravery and adventure.

The most clearly marked differences in the dreams of these children, as compared with those of normal children are :—

(1) The greater number of dreams of the clearly defined wish-fulfilment type. Nearly half the dreams are of this nature.

(2) The extraordinarily close approximation of the proportion of the wish-fulfilment dreams, fear dreams, and kinæsthetic dreams of the boys to those of the girls.

(3) The fulfilled wishes are of a very special type, consisting principally of dreams of home life ; of visits of parents to the school ; of large parcels from home, containing many presents ; of changes of fortune ; of success in life ; of deeds of valour and promotion to positions of great responsibility. The industrial school child is a most ambitious and imaginative dreamer.

(4) The fear dreams are very similar among boys and girls. The boy, however, especially at the age of fourteen, dreams more of ghosts, and at all ages the girl dreams more of houses on fire.

(5) A very marked difference is to be observed in the kinæsthetic dreams. The proportion among boys and girls is practically the same, but they are much less frequent

than among normal children. It would appear that the regular life of the institution is not conducive to this type of dream.

(6) The family group take comparatively little part in the dreams, their place being taken by the boy's chum and the girl's particular friend. The proportion of some-one other than the chief figure taking part in the dream is about the same as in the dreams of normal children.

Although among the main group of dream elements the proportions approximate so closely in the boys and girls, there are minor points in which they differ considerably. The more important are :—

(1) Girls dream far more about school activities than boys.

(2) The boys have three times as many dreams of bravery and adventure as the girls, but the girls have far more than those of the elementary school.

(3) Fairy stories are still prominent in the girls', but are practically non-existent in the boys' dreams.

(4) Conversations occur in boys' more often than in girls' dreams.

(5) The death element rarely comes into

the dreams, but is more common among boys than among girls.

(6) The boy occasionally dreams of thefts, in which he or his chum takes an active part, but this element does not appear in girls' dreams.

As typical of industrial school dreams the following may be mentioned :—

DREAMS OF SUCCESS IN LIFE

(*a*) *A boy of* 12 :

I dreamt I left this school, and had a good situation as an engineer. I dreamt that after a long time I rose to be chief engineer and that I was rolling in money. One day, when I was instructing some men about machinery, I was informed that a gentleman wished to converse with me. When he was in my office I was astonished to see that he was my own superintendent, but what made me startled was that he asked me for employment. He said he knew a considerable amount about mechanics. I knew I was short of men, so I employed him as my own chauffeur.

(*b*) *A boy of* 14 :

My last dream was of motors, motor

bicycles and aeroplanes, all of which I thought I possessed. I went into business with the idea of becoming like Selfridges and to possess everything. I first had a motor bicycle, which I bought very cheaply, but thought a motor better, so I bought one. I always carried my motor bicycle at the back of my car. One day I met a nice young lady but before long forgot about her. My business becoming great I bought an aeroplane. I had many trips in my aeroplane, the greatest being to Australia. I started from London and while above sea I saw a U boat and many other ships. While in Australia I set up another business and at last became a millionaire. I asked my mother to come across but she would not, so I went to her. Until this time I did not possess a house but after trouble I saw a beautiful large mansion and bought it. Having nothing to do I became a doctor and became renowned for my being able to cure the influenza.

FAIRY-STORY DREAM

A girl of 12 :

Last night I had a most strange dream. I dreamt that sister gave me some money

G

and I went to a shop and bought a chocolate nurse and took it home with me and laid it in the cupboard. When tea-time came I sat down at the table and waited to be served. Just at that moment the chocolate nurse came walking out of the cupboard and served me with my tea. I thought this very strange but after a while I began talking to it. At night I made a little bed for it in the doll's house. Next morning she served me with my breakfast and after that I took her for a nice walk in the meadows to pick flowers. There were some cows feeding in the meadow and one of them ate poor chocolate nurse. I then woke up.

DOMESTIC DREAMS

(a) *A girl of* 13 :

I dreamt that we had a party and we invited some outside people, the Kaiser and Prince Willie were there; I was sitting on the fender by the prince and three of my friends. The gramophone was playing and we were told to get up and dance, so my three friends pushed me out to dance with the prince and we were dancing and the people were having a good laugh at us.

(*b*) *A boy of* 13 :

I dreamt that I went home for three weeks. The first day I went to my sister's house and she let me sleep in her bed. She gave me some money, cake and some toffee. The next week I went to my uncle's house and he said that I had grown and that I was very fat. I slept in his house for eleven days. It was my birthday on the seventh day so my uncle gave me a pony and a cart. I had a long ride home again and showed them to my mother, father and the children, and my father said that he would buy me a motor and my mother said she would buy me a silver watch and chain. Just then someone made a noise and woke me up.

BRAVERY AND ADVENTURE

(*a*) *A boy of* 14 :

Last night I dreamt about a journey over to Germany in an aeroplane. I went over to Germany to kill the Kaiser. In my journey I passed many wonderful sights. After many adventures I reached Germany. As I was flying over Germany I spotted the Kaiser's house and dropped a bomb on it. It happened to be that the Kaiser was inside it. It blew him to pieces and all that was in it. After that I was getting ready to go back to England. I was returning back when seven German aeroplanes chased me. They levelled with me so I had to fight them, in which I was victorious. When I got back to England I was rewarded with the Victoria Cross for being victor of the battle with the seven German aeroplanes and £1,000 for the death of the Kaiser. I was just having the Victoria Cross and the £1,000 when I heard a voice and it said, " Turn out of bed."

(*b*) *A boy of* 14 :

I dreamt that I went to live in Australia, and while I was there a gold mine was found, and crowds of people flocked to the mine and I was with them. When we had been waiting there a long time a big wealthy man came out whom I guessed was the manager. He was dressed in a big tweed suit and a gold watch and chain on his waistcoat. He walked about the men, picking out the men he needed and I was one of them. When he had got our names we began to build our huts, two men to each hut. Next day we went down into the mine with our picks and shovels and began to work. When we came to the gold it was taken up to the top and stored in a little hut. When we had finished the day's work my companion says to me, "We'll get some of that gold and clear off to-night and we will take it to my home." That night we got some gold and took it to his home; while I was there I heard him say to his wife, "We'll do away with this chap." So in the night I got up, took the gold and made tracks for home.

FEAR DREAM

A girl of 14 :

I dreamt I heard scratching, and then a very large black rat rushed across the dormitory. It chased us up one flight of stairs and down the other. Just as we were running along the top passage a train came upstairs. The rat pushed us all in and very soon we came to Victoria Station. Here we tried to get out, but there were no doors, so the rat made holes in the top of the train and we jumped out. As the rat came on to the platform it changed into a man. We were very frightened of him.

In industrial schools many boys of thirteen and fourteen dream of joining the Air Force.

There are very few neurotic dreams among the girls ; they are generally very imaginative but quite healthy.   Among the girls thieving very rarely comes into the dream, and of twenty-three cases recorded in the boys' dreams there appeared to be only one case for which there was any consciousness of wrong : stealing in the industrial boy's dream is simply a normal form of adventure.

Among the more vivid dreamers were :—

(*a*) A girl of fifteen who dreamt of a real storm of living cats and dogs.

(*b*) A boy of twelve who has a conversation with a worm with a large head.   On cutting off the head, the tail pursued the terrified boy, shouting, " Give me back my head."

(*c*) A girl of eleven who describing her own funeral, at which she was an onlooker, criticised adversely the wreath which was sent by her schoolfellows.

(*d*) A boy of twelve who dreamt that his mother was converted into a china ornament which was accidentally broken.

In industrial schools the conditions of life

of the boy and girl approximate far more closely than those of normal children attending day schools, and it is very interesting to observe, as seen in the results of the analyses, the effect upon the dream ; the remarkable similarity in many important elements, especially as regards wish-fulfilment, fear and kinæsthetic dreams.

Another reason for the extraordinary interest of the dreams of these children is that they have been thrown so much upon their own resources and have passed through such a variety of experiences that the content of the unconscious is far richer than that of the normal child who has led an uneventful and fully protected existence. The difference can be seen at once by a comparison of their dreams with those of children of the same age in different types of schools as shown by the illustrative examples in the earlier chapters. In some cases the dreams in their richness of material and effective combinations are years ahead of those of normal children. This becomes more striking still when it is remembered how unfavourable is the nomadic life for acquiring the educational background needed for graphic description in the recording of dreams. It would seem to indicate that there is an abnormal amount of natural ability in the children of the industrial schools.

CHAPTER VII

DREAMS OF DEAF AND BLIND CHILDREN

THERE are very clearly marked differences in the dreams of deaf and blind children. The deaf child can draw upon a rich field of visual experiences which, in their fantastic combinations, give such a wealth of interest to the dream ; whereas these experiences are wanting in the dream of the child who has been blind from birth.

The percentage of clearly defined wish-fulfilments in both types of child corresponds closely to that of normal children, but the wishes are of a different nature. Concerts, parties, and domestic experience bulk largely in the dreams of the blind child, and there is not that variety which corresponds to the much fuller life of the deaf child. In the latter, visits of the town child to the country form, especially among older children, a very important item, whereas in the former, there are practically no references to such experiences. The railway journey, the change of scene, and even the seaside have no message for the blind child.

The fears of the deaf and blind are somewhat in excess of those of normal children. In both the fear of animals is greater than among ordinary children, and in the case of the deaf it is twice as great as in that of the blind. The fear of fire is far greater among the blind, particularly in young children, than in any other type of child. The air raid also had a much greater terror for the blind child than for normal children. A year after the last raid it formed an unwelcome element in a large percentage of his dreams. On the whole, blind children, especially up to the age of twelve years, dream far less than deaf children, but this was not true at the time of the air raids.

It is interesting to observe that, whilst among blind children the proportion of kinæsthetic dreams for the same age is very considerably below that of normal seeing children, this type of dream is practically non-existent among deaf children.

Bravery and adventure figure very prominently in the dreams of deaf girls, far more so than in the dreams 'of girls in elementary and secondary schools. Associated with this it is interesting to note that the air raid has left practically no trace on the dream of the deaf girl. The deaf girl, in fact, in her love of bravery and adventure, approximates closely to the elementary school boy of the same age. Bravery and adventure have no place in the dream of the blind child. The fairy story makes a much stronger appeal to the deaf than to the blind girl.

Dreams in which conversations are recorded are in about the same proportion among blind as among normal children ; but in deaf children they are far more common, the relative number being thirteen to five.

The family group or special friends enter into the dreams of both blind and deaf children in much the same proportion as in those of ordinary children.

The difference between the dreams of deaf and blind children is seen in the following examples :—

Deaf Children

DOMESTIC DREAMS

(*a*) *A boy of* 12 :

One night I dreamt of a foot. I thought it was lying down on the floor and I, not expecting such a thing, fell over it. It seemed to be the same shape as my own foot. The foot suddenly jumped up and started running after me ; I thought I jumped right through the window, ran round the yard out into the street and running along as fast as my legs would carry me. I thought I ran to Woolwich, and then it suddenly caught me and shook me, and then I woke up. I have dreamt about this foot several times.

NOTE.—This boy's father was a sailor and met with an accident at sea, breaking his ankle.

(*b*) *A girl of* 15 (*deaf from birth*) :

I dreamt that I dressed properly and went out for a walk. A nice boy came to me and said, " Would you like to be my sweetheart ? " I said yes, and he took me to the picture palace. Next day he knocked at my door. I opened the door, and shook hands with him and said, " come in." He sat down in the parlour; I put my hat and coat on and went out for a walk. I said to him, "Do you want some tea with me?" He said, "Yes, please." We had bread and butter and jam, breakfast biscuits and cakes and tea. I washed the things up and I put on my hat and coat and went out to church about seven o'clock. He asked me, "Would you like to marry me next Sunday?" I said, "Yes please." He bought some wedding cake with ice on it and a wedding ring. Next Saturday I made a veil for myself. On the wedding day he came home. The motor car came to my house. He took my arm and we went in the motor to church. He gave me a ring and kissed me, and Harry, Mother, Father, and the children.

BRAVERY AND ADVENTURE

(a) A girl of 16 *(deaf for* 9 *years):*

On Saturday night I dreamt I was a hearing girl and I was an airwoman. I flew over Germany and stole some German secret plans. I flew back to England again and gave the plans to Mr. Lloyd George. The people cheered me because the plans were about the Peace Terms, and in the next week the war came to an end and peace was signed.   I thought my story was printed in a newspaper, which said I brought this war to an end.   I was cheered by the people again and woke when I saw a German fire a shot at me.

(b) *A girl of* 16 (*deaf from birth*) :

Last night I dreamt that I went for a walk and I saw a big aeroplane and the airmen went to a shop to buy something. Then I went into the aeroplane and I flew straight from Oxford Street to Berlin.   I saw a lot of Germans marching about, and I went down to the ground.   One of them was dead and I took the German's coat, trousers, cap and gun and wore them.   I saw the Germans drinking beer and I went into a big building, where I saw a lot of British soldiers in the prison.   They were very unhappy because they wanted to eat and drink.   Then two of the Germans went to sleep behind the prison and I took a pair of boots and I took the guns and a big key and I told the British soldiers that I was an English girl.   They were very glad.   When it was dark I opened the door and they followed me, and I gave them the Germans' horses.   They had all gone except me.   Next morning the Germans were very surprised and they told the Kaiser about the prisoners. Then he was very angry with them. One night I went to a private room and I wanted to find a secret paper. At last I found it in the Kaiser's case. Suddenly the Germans saw me and caught me, but I ate the piece of paper. Then they took me to the Kaiser and he was very angry with me and put me in the prison. The British soldiers never heard about me and they thought that the Germans had caught me. Next day the Kaiser told the Germans to shoot me because I ate the secret paper; then they shot me. The Allies captured the Germans but they could not find me. One of the soldiers found me in a room and carried me to a motor and sent me to the hospital in France and the doctor said that I was a brave girl because I ate the secret paper.

Blind Children

FEAR DREAMS

(a) *A boy of* 11 :

One night I had a dream. I thought I saw a great rat making a large hole in our bedroom floor. When he had made a hole large enough for him to get through he called six other rats. I seemed to imagine they were going to take refuge in the fire-place. Then I thought I saw a cat come into the room. As soon as the rats heard the cat they fled away. Then I woke to find it was morning.

(*b*) *A girl of* 11 :

I dreamt I was having a bath when one of our matrons told me to go into the dining-room to get a doll and pram for one of the children. She told me that I need not put my shoes and stockings on, so I went into the dining-room, and I was so frightened because I thought I saw a lot of mice and beetles running after me, and I thought they were biting me. And I was crying and screaming and I said I would not go into the dining-room again at night. When I woke up there were tears on my pillow where I had been crying.

(*c*) *A girl of* 13 :

I dreamt I was playing in the play-ground with a long rope. My little sister and big sister were up the other end of the playground. In came a big black dog and came up to me. I was frightened so I ran up to my sister and the dog followed me. Then we walked up the playground to go into the school. The dog came up

to me and said, "How do you do, Annie?"
But I did not answer. He asked me again
and again, but I would not answer him.
So he went round to my little sister and
said, "How do you do, Winnie?" She
said, "Quite well, thank you." He said,
"Annie will not speak to me." When we
went into the school we shut the doors so
that the dog could not get in. But the
dog pulled them open again. Then the
dog asked me to sit down with him to
have a talk. But I would not, so he asked
my sister Winnie, and she went and sat
down with him. There was a lady and the
cook and my sister talking about what
they could do with him. Then the lady
said, "Cut off his head." Then we said,
"Hush, because he can hear you." The
cook went to get a knife, but the dog
escaped. That night when I was in bed
the girls said, "There is a big brown dog
come in the front gate." It was night, but
all the girls were sitting up in bed eating
their dinner. Then the dog came up to
me and started jumping up to me. Then
I jumped up in bed and woke up.

(d) *A boy of* 14 :

I was sound asleep in bed when I was
awakened by my mother who shouted
"Quick, Frank! the house is on fire."

H

I was up in an instant and was trying to dress myself when my mother caught hold of me and forced her way down the stairs. It was too late. The flames had hold of us and as I was burning I could hear the voices of the people and my mother's voice gradually fading and my body was all alight.

Just as I was feeling the flames catch my hair something went "bang"! and immediately I awoke.

(e) *A boy of* 14:

One night I dreamed that our school was on fire. The bells rang all over the building telling us that something was wrong. The master came in and told us all to keep calm and get dressed quickly. When we were dressed we got our partners and went down to the lawn.

Then the fire brigade came and they asked some of the boys to help them to hold the water pipes. Then we were taken into the gymnasium so that we should not take cold. The gas was turned off for safety. The fire lasted about three hours. The firemen went away but we could not sleep in the house. Some blankets had been salved so we had one each and went to sleep in the gymnasium.

DOMESTIC DREAM

A girl of 13 :

One night I had a most peculiar dream. I dreamt that my sister was getting married. In the other part of the house I dreamt that there was a funeral. I could not make out who the person was who was being buried in the part of the house where the funeral was being carried out. The wedding service was in the same church as the funeral service. The people in the wedding and the people in the funeral were reversed. The people in the funeral were very happy and the people in the wedding who ought to have been happy were very disappointed and solemn.

The bravery and adventure dreams of deaf girls, generally take the form of the dreamers acting as airwomen and frequently as spies. A girl of fifteen and her friend go to the Western Front disguised as Germans, set free a number of British prisoners, kill the Kaiser and are presented with medals by the King. Another girl kills the Kaiser and is congratulated by British officers, who give her ten medals.

Deaf girls dream much of personal adornment, which is entirely lacking in dreams of blind girls.

Many blind children claim to see in their dreams. A girl of fourteen says, "I can always see in my dreams. I have never yet had a dream without seeing quite plainly." But the dreams recorded are generally of an uneventful nature dealing with domestic incidents in which vision takes no part. There are many auditory dreams and a few taste dreams. In the deaf child's dream descriptions of the clothes worn by the actors frequently occur, but these are rarely to be found in the dreams of the blind; and there is scarcely ever any mention of colour, although some blind children associate special colours with particular objects.

Deaf children also state that in their dreams they hear clearly, and, as has been pointed out, the accounts of their dreams contain more definite conversations than those of any other type of child. The more intelligent blind children take great interest in the books specially prepared for them. An account of *Lorna Doone* in which the child took one of the characters in the book in her dream was of unusual interest. Blind children form great friendships with girls at the same school, and in their dreams it is frequently the girl friend who is present rather than members of the family group.

There is no evidence whatever in the dreams analysed that a child blind from birth ever sees as a dreamer, but there is abundant evidence that those who have recently become blind see clearly. The age of becoming blind appears to be the deciding factor. Jastrow and Heerman investigated this point fully. Their researches point to the conclusions—

(1) That a child who becomes blind before the age of five never sees in his dreams.

(2) That when total blindness occurs between the ages of five and seven, much depends on the mental development of the child as to whether he sees in dreams in after life or not. The well-developed child mentally certainly does; the evidence with regard to the others is not so clear.

(3) That all dreamers becoming blind after the age of seven see in dreams even after an

interval of twenty or thirty years; and apparently with little diminution in clearness.

These conclusions are well established. The question with regard to the partially blind seeing more clearly in dreams than in waking life is more open to doubt.

CHAPTER VIII

EDUCATIONAL VALUE OF THE DREAM

REFERENCES have already been made (1) to the great value of the dream in the diagnosis of mental diseases ; and (2) to the great difference that exists between the dreams of children and those of neurotic adults, or even those of normal adults. The question now arises, to what extent the dream of the child may yield such additional information to that previously possessed as will be of value to the teacher ? It is suggested that a careful study of children's dreams may throw much light on the special interests and desires of the child at different ages, and, especially where persistent dreams are recorded of unfulfilled wishes, on those elements which are conspicuously lacking in the life of the child and which may seriously interfere with his natural development. The most obvious of these are dreams which indicate underfeeding and those which give evidence of undue stress and strain.

The normal child thoroughly enjoys school life, but not infrequently cases are found in which the child, for no obvious reason, is absolutely out of harmony with his surroundings. He is not lacking in ability, is apparently healthy, and has definite out-of-school interests, but his life in school is one of continual opposition to authority. The dreams of this type of difficult child would be of special interest and might be of the greatest value, not only in indicating some particular line of possible development, but also in throwing light upon any special feature wanting in his environment. The weakly, neurotic child would naturally be dealt with by the medical officer or the psycho-analyst. A special study of children's fears at different ages would also be of considerable value, but for this purpose dreams should be recorded at regular intervals. Thus, in a variety of ways in the normal life of the school, much useful information may be obtained by a study of children's dreams which cannot be secured so well by any other method.

There are many important problems, however, which appear to open up great possibilities in the child's dream as an object of research. From various sources there comes a large body of evidence as to the very great influence the unconscious exerts in every department of mental activity, and a fuller knowledge of the unconscious is as essential in dealing with the normal development of children as in the abnormal cases in which it has proved to be of such extraordinary value. If this be true, then the dream as the best means of investigating the unconscious must play a very important rôle in the educational developments of the future.

Although the unconscious in the past has received far less attention than it deserves, every student of child nature has felt that in the mental make-up of the child there is some very powerful influence at work over which he has no control, and the action of which in affecting the child's behaviour under varying conditions he cannot successfully prophesy.

The mystery of mysteries in education is the prodigious progress made by the intelligent child during the period of five to nine years of age, a rate of progress in mental achievement out of all proportion to that of any other period of life. It cannot be explained by the intense interest in life and the retentive memory of a child at this age. It is not only in mental content that the advance is so marked, there is also a power of dealing with the acquired material which points clearly to the drawing on reserves of which we have only an imperfect knowledge.

In this connection, much insight into the child mind can be obtained by a study of children's essays on subjects in which they are deeply interested and have first-hand knowledge, and in which, moreover, they are describing their own experiences. Their power of graphic description—of conciseness in expression—of dramatic record of events—and frequently of excellent construction of difficult sentences, make it almost impossible to regard the result as the unaided work of an immature child. A similar confirmation of the remarkable, almost uncanny, ability of young children can be obtained by conversation under favourable circumstances. Experience shows that for this purpose it is better to have two intelligent children together, unless the observer is on sufficiently good terms with the observed to be regarded for the time being as an intelligent child. Any pretension to superiority is fatal. Surround the children with novel objects of great interest—a first visit to a Natural History Museum generally satisfies the condition—and then let them give their own impressions of what they see. Such an experiment is most illuminating. Investigations of this type prove beyond doubt the existence of the reserves of which I have spoken. The records of dreams of which examples are given in the preceding chapters were selected for a special purpose, but some of them indicate a standard of achievement considerably beyond the normal for children of the stated age. Some of the others which are not quoted were remarkable performances for quite young children. A distinguished authority has stated that "the dramatic power of a dunce in dreaming exceeds that which is displayed by the most imaginative writer in his waking state."

If the content of the unconscious consists of the racial inheritance in addition to repressed material of a personal character, it would be reasonable to suppose that the unconscious of the young child would in much larger proportion consist of the former element and that the contributions from this source would be much richer than to those of riper years. It is also reasonable to suppose that the racial inheritance would be the dominating factor in that general ability which varies to such a great extent in children. This variation can be clearly seen in any group of very young children of the same age. It would appear, therefore, that a knowledge of the unconscious of the child is a matter of prime importance, and that the dream should be fully utilised for the purpose of gaining as much information about it as is possible.

Valuable contributions from the unconscious to the affairs of everyday life are by no means confined to children. There is an increasing mass of evidence that some of the finest creations in literature have had their origin in dreams. Robert Louis Stevenson in " A Chapter on Dreams " speaks in unqualified terms of his great indebtedness to the unconscious for valuable material supplied to him in dreams, which he has simply elaborated and developed to the great delight of his readers. He states that the basis of most of his stories came as ideas and suggestions from the world of dreams. Similar evidence can be obtained from a variety of sources. Many reliable records are also available of the solution of problems, the clearing up of difficult situations and matters of a similar nature through the action of the unconscious working through the dream. When confronted with a position of unusual complexity, on which a decision must be reached, the general desire to "sleep over it" is full of significance.

As a result of an investigation of dreams carried out with unusual thoroughness and care, De Sanctis came to the conclusion that dream life is a revelation of individual character. This is especially the case with young children. The dream lets in a flood of light as to the temperament and mental make-up of the child ; it may also indicate the presence of repressed material in the unconscious.

Of recent years much patient research has been carried on with excellent results in the investigation of the effect of repressed material in the unconscious of neurotics, and, for a different purpose, equally good results may possibly be obtained by the study of repressed material in children. It might incidentally result in the avoidance of educational methods which are favourable to repression—*e.g.*, the absence of opportunity for a natural, strong interest to develop in a child may lead to serious results. The evil effect of certain repressed material in the unconscious, makes it imperative that nothing in the general scheme of education should lead to such repression. The Montessori method owes much of its undoubted success to the insistence on the free and natural mental growth of a developing child along the line of its main interests.

For Product Safety Concerns and Information please contact our EU
representative GPSR@taylorandfrancis.com
Taylor & Francis Verlag GmbH, Kaufingerstraße 24, 80331 München, Germany

www.ingramcontent.com/pod-product-compliance
Lightning Source LLC
Chambersburg PA
CBHW050534270326
41926CB00015B/3217

9 780367 109493